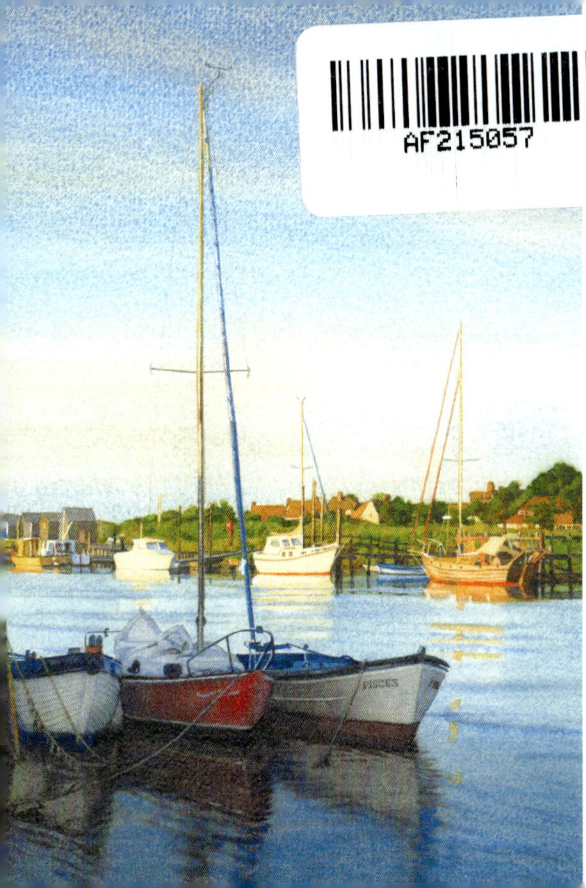

FAVOURITE FISH and SEAFOOD RECIPES

from Britain's Coastal Waters

illustrated by
Margaret Heath RSMA

Dorrigo

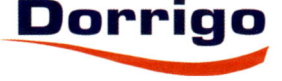

Index

Baked Cod with Savoury Tomato Sauce 21
Braised Herrings 11
Creamy Cheese Haddock 31
Creamy Finnan Haddie 29
Creamy Stuffed Plaice 10
Crispy Battered Cod 7
Crumbed Cod Fingers 43
Crunchy Baked Fish 16
Cullen Skink 35
Dorset Crab Tart 40
Dover Sole 14
Fish and Vegetable Stew 26
Fish Cobbler 8
Fish Hotpot 47
Fish Soup 22
Fish Stuffed Pancakes 30
Fish Supper 32

Fisherman's Pie 6
Haddock in Lemon Butter Sauce 46
Kedgeree 19
Lyme Bay Fish Pie 18
Mackerel in Cider and Apple Sauce 5
Monkfish Casserole 15
Plaice and Prawn Supreme 42
Potted Shrimps 13
Roast Sea Bass 45
Savoury Fish Crumble 38
Savoury Plaice Mornay 27
Skate with Black Butter 23
Soused Herrings 37
Spiced Cod 34
Stuffed Sole 3
Sussex Lobster or Crab Pie 24
Whiting and Bacon Whirls 39

Stuffed Sole

A tasty dish for a dinner party and an excellent meal for Good Friday
when it is traditional not to eat meat

2 hard boiled eggs, peeled and chopped   8 oz. peeled cooked prawns
Fresh dill – 1 teaspoon chopped and a few sprigs for garnishing
4 large sole fillets   1 oz. butter   2 spring onions, chopped
5 fl. oz. dry white vermouth   2 egg yolks   ¼ pint double cream
1½ tablespoons concentrated tomato purée   Salt & pepper

Mix the chopped egg, prawns, chopped onions and dill together and spread this mixture over one half of each sole fillet. Fold the uncovered half of each fillet over the top of the stuffing and place into a large non-stick frying pan. Put a small knob of butter on top of each and pour over the vermouth. Place the pan on a gentle heat and allow to come to the boil. Cover the pan tightly and allow to simmer gently for 10-15 minutes, until the sole is cooked, ensuring that the filling has warmed through. Remove from the pan using a fish slice, transferring to a warm serving plate. Meanwhile, mix together the tomato purée, egg yolks and double cream until smooth. Add to the pan juices, heating gently and stirring continuously until thickened. (Do not allow to boil or the sauce may curdle.) Season to taste, pour around fish, garnish with dill sprigs and serve. Serves 4.

Mackerel in Cider and Apple Sauce

Mackerel is best eaten very fresh. With its characteristic blue-black markings, a creamy coloured flesh and a distinctive flavour, it is in season from October to July.

**1 oz. butter   ½ onion, finely chopped   1 tablespoon cornflour
4 mackerel, filleted   ¾ pint dry cider   1 bay leaf
Salt & pepper to season
2 small dessert apples, peeled, cored and sliced thinly**

Melt the butter in a large non-stick frying pan, add the onion and cook until translucent. Add the cornflour and cook for 1 minute stirring continuously. Slowly add the cider whilst continuing to stir. Season to taste and add the mackerel fillets. Cover tightly, reduce the heat and allow to simmer gently for 15 minutes until the mackerel is tender. Remove mackerel and keep warm. Turn up the heat slightly, add the apple slices to the pan and simmer for 4-5 minutes until the sauce is thick and reduced. Pour the sauce over the fish and serve. Serves 4.

"Lady Irene", Deal Beach, Kent

Fisherman's Pie

A hearty family meal of creamy mashed potato and tender fish in white sauce.

Topping:
2 lb. potatoes   Large knob of butter   3 tablespoons milk   Salt and pepper to season
Filling:
¾ lb. skinned smoked haddock fillet, cubed   ¾ lb. skinned cod fillet, cubed
2 tablespoons dill chopped and a few sprigs to garnish   A few drops of tabasco sauce
½ lb. young spinach leaves   4 large tomatoes   2 oz. grated Cheddar cheese
Sauce:
1 oz. butter   1 oz. cornflour   ¼ pint milk   ¼ pint soured cream

Set oven to 350ºF or Mark 4. Boil potatoes in salted water until soft. Drain and mash with milk, butter and seasoning until creamy. (More milk can be added if required.) Blanch spinach leaves in boiling water for 2 minutes then drain well. To make the sauce, melt butter in a saucepan, add flour and cook, stirring well for 1 minute. Away from the heat, add milk and cream slowly, stirring to ensure they are well mixed. Return pan to the heat, stirring until thickened, then add the fish, chopped dill and tabasco sauce. Slice tomatoes and cover the bottom of an ovenproof dish with half of them followed by half the spinach. Layer fish mixture over this and top with the rest of the tomatoes and spinach. Pipe the potato to cover and grate the cheese over the top. Bake in oven for 30 minutes, garnish and serve with green salad. Serves 4.

Crispy Battered Cod

The bubbles from the lager make the batter crisp, but it must be used immediately.

4 medium cod fillets
5 oz. self-raising flour plus extra for dusting fillets
½ pint lager
Vegetable oil for deep frying
Salt and freshly ground black pepper

Gently heat the oil in a deep frying pan. Season the fish fillets with salt and pepper, and dust lightly with flour. Sieve the rest of the flour and salt into a mixing bowl. Make a well in the centre and gently pour in the lager, whisking together to make a smooth, thick and frothy pouring batter. Use the batter straight away. Dip the pre-floured fillets of fish into the batter and lower into the hot fat. Fry for 7-8 minutes until golden and crisp. Remove using a slotted spoon/slice and drain on kitchen paper. Serves 4.

Fish Cobbler

The scone topping on this dish mounds up to look somewhat like cobblestones.

1½ lb. cod or haddock 1 pint milk 1 bay leaf 2 oz. butter 2 oz. flour
1 onion, skinned and diced 4 oz. peeled prawns 1 tablespoon chopped fresh parsley
Juice of ½ lemon Salt and pepper
Scone Topping:
8 oz. self-raising flour Pinch salt 1 level teaspoon baking powder
1 level teaspoon dry mustard powder 2 oz. butter
3 oz. Wensleydale cheese, grated 1 egg, beaten Nearly ¼ pint milk

Set oven to 425°F or Mark 7. Cook fish in a pan with half the milk and bay leaf; do not overcook. Reserve the liquid, skin and flake the fish. Melt the butter in a pan, stir in the flour and cook without browning, stirring all the time for 2-3 minutes. Remove from the heat, stir in the fish liquid and remaining milk. Return to the heat and bring to the boil, stirring continuously. When sauce thickens add onion and cook gently for 5 minutes. Remove from heat and add fish, prawns, parsley and lemon juice, seasoning well. Put into a 2½ pint ovenproof dish. Make scone topping: place dry ingredients, except cheese, in a bowl. Rub in butter, stir in cheese, add egg and sufficient milk to make a soft dough. Knead lightly, roll out to ½ inch thick and cut into small scones. Arrange overlapping around the edge of fish mixture. Bake for 10-15 minutes until scones are risen and golden brown.

Evening at Holywell Bay, Cornwall

Creamy Stuffed Plaice

An elegant supper dish of plaice fillets filled with a tasty bacon and mushroom stuffing.

1 lb. potatoes, peeled and chopped	3 oz. sliced mushrooms
Salt & pepper	4 rashers lean bacon, chopped
2 oz. butter	5 fl. oz. double cream
4 large plaice fillets, skinned	Parsley to garnish

Set oven to 375°F or Mark 5. Cook potatoes in salted water until soft. Mash with 1 oz. butter and season to taste. Put into a piping bag and pipe around edge of a shallow ovenproof dish. Heat rest of butter in a frying pan and add mushrooms and bacon. Cook until softened and slightly browned. Spoon onto fillets and roll up from tail to head, using a cocktail stick to secure. Put into ovenproof dish. Add seasoning to the cream and pour over the fish. Cover with foil and bake in preheated oven for 15 minutes until the fish is softened. Remove foil lid and cocktail sticks and garnish with the parsley. Serves 4.

Braised Herrings

Herring has been a known staple food source since 3000 B.C. Very high in healthy oils, there are numerous ways to serve herrings and many regional recipes.

**½ bottle red wine   1 onion, peeled and thickly sliced
2 carrots, peeled and thickly sliced   1 stick of celery, roughly chopped
1 bay leaf   4 peppercorns   A bouquet garni
Salt & pepper to season
4 herrings, cleaned and heads, tails and fins removed**

Set oven to 325°F or Mark 3. Put the sliced vegetables, bay leaf, peppercorns, herbs and seasoning with the wine into a saucepan. Cover and simmer gently for ½ hour. Lay herrings in the bottom of an ovenproof dish. Strain the wine liquor over them ensuring the herrings are covered. A little water may be added if necessary. Cover and cook in the preheated oven for about 1 hour. Serve with cooking liquid. Serves 4.

Potted Shrimps

Morecambe Bay shrimps – small and brown – are considered to be among the finest in the country and have been popular since the 18th century.

1 lb. shelled shrimps or prawns	**½ teaspoon mace**
6 oz. butter	**Pinch of cayenne pepper**
1 to 2 teaspoons anchovy essence	**Salt**

Set oven to 325°F or Mark 3. Cut the shrimps or prawns in half. In a saucepan melt 4 oz. of the butter with the anchovy essence, spices and salt. Put the shrimps or prawns in an ovenproof dish, pour the butter mixture over, cover and cook in the oven for 15 to 20 minutes. Drain the shrimps or prawns well, reserving the butter mixture and pack into small jars or moulds. Strain the reserved butter mixture and pour over the shrimps or prawns, dividing it evenly. Leave to set. Melt the remaining 2 oz. butter and pour onto the jars or moulds to seal the mixture. Place in the refrigerator overnight before serving. Serve with brown bread or fingers of toast. Serves 4-6.

Dover Sole with watercress and anchovy butter

Dover sole is known as one of the kings among fish.
Its delicate flavour and lightly textured flesh holds together when cut into.

8 fillets of sole, skinned	**2 oz. unsalted butter, softened**
A bunch of watercress	**1 teaspoon anchovy essence**
	½ lemon

Set oven to 350°F or Mark 4. Grease an ovenproof dish. Season the fillets with pepper and lemon juice, then roll each one up and place side by side, join side down, in the dish. Sprinkle with a little more lemon juice, and then cover with greased foil. Cook in the oven for 15-20 minutes. Meanwhile trim the watercress, reserving a few sprigs for garnish, and blanch in boiling water for 1 minute. Refresh it under cold water, and then drain it. Chop the cress finely and blend with the butter and anchovy essence. This can be done in a blender. Form into 8 'pats' and leave in a cool place until needed. Place the cooked fillets on a warm dish, garnish with the reserved sprigs of watercress and serve with the pats of watercress butter. Serves 4.

Monkfish Casserole

With its succulent, firm texture and slightly sweet flavour, monkfish is highly sought after by fishermen in the waters around South-west England.

**1½ pints dry cider   1 oz. butter   1 large onion, peeled and diced
4 oz. button mushrooms   1½ lb monkfish, skinned and cut into cubes
1 oz. flour   1 tablespoon fresh parsley, finely chopped
1 teaspoon marjoram, finely chopped   Salt and pepper
2 tablespoons single cream**

Set oven to 325°F or Mark 3. Boil the cider rapidly in a saucepan to reduce it to 1 pint. In a separate pan melt the butter, add the onion and cook for 3 minutes. Add the mushrooms and fish and cook for 1 minute, then add the flour and stir well. Pour the cider over, stir well and add the herbs. Season to taste. Transfer to a casserole dish and bake for 30 minutes (or continue to cook on top of the cooker for 30 minutes). Stir in the cream just before serving. Serve with fresh vegetables and crusty bread. Serves 4.

Crunchy Baked Fish

A simple, tasty and healthy way to cook fish. Any white fish may be used.

1½ lb. white fish fillet, skinned   Salt & freshly milled black pepper
3 oz. butter   1 egg yolk   2 tablespoons chopped flat leaf parsley
3 oz. dried breadcrumbs   5 fl. oz. dry cider or white wine
4 medium tomatoes, halved

Set oven to 450°F or Mark 8. Cut fish into 4 pieces and season with salt and pepper. Place fillets in greased ovenproof dish. Cream together 2 oz. of butter and egg yolk. Add parsley and mix well. Spread mixture evenly over fillets, sprinkle with breadcrumbs and dot with pieces of remaining butter. Pour the cider around the fish and bake in the oven for 20 minutes. Place the halved tomatoes between the fish and return to oven for a further 5 minutes. Garnish with sprigs of parsley and serve with new potatoes and green vegetables. Serves 4.

Low Tide at Wells-next-the-Sea, Norfolk

Lyme Bay Fish Pie

A luxury fish pie filling topped with filo pastry; not at all like an ordinary fish pie.

8 oz. filo pastry   2 oz. butter   6 spring onions, trimmed and sliced
4 oz. mushrooms, wiped and sliced   1 oz. plain flour
½ pint fish stock   ¼ pint dry white wine
8 oz. white fish fillets, skinned and cut into pieces
8 oz. scallops   8 oz. prawns, cooked and peeled (thaw if frozen)
4 tomatoes, skinned, de-seeded and cut into strips
1 tablespoon chopped parsley   Salt and pepper

Set oven to 375°F or Mark 5. Melt 1 oz. butter in a large frying pan and gently cook the onions and mushrooms for 3 to 4 minutes. Stir in the flour and cook for 2 to 3 minutes. Remove from the heat and add the stock gradually, stirring well all the time. Stir in the wine. Return to the heat and bring to the boil; cook for 3 to 4 minutes. Remove from the heat and add the fish pieces, scallops, prawns, tomatoes and parsley. Season and put into a shallow ovenproof dish. Melt the remaining butter in a small pan. Arrange the sheets of filo pastry on top of the fish, brushing each layer with melted butter. Trim the pastry and score the surface into diamond shapes. Cook for 25 to 30 minutes until golden. Serve hot. Serves 4.

Kedgeree

Kedgeree was typically served as a breakfast dish during Victorian times.
Now it makes a good lunch or tasty supper dish.

6 oz. long grain rice
4 hard boiled eggs, chopped finely
1 lb. smoked haddock, cooked

1 onion, finely chopped
4 oz. butter or margarine
1 tablespoon chopped parsley

2 tablespoons single cream

(To cook fish – put in a pan, cover with cold water, cover with a lid. Bring to boil slowly, turn off heat and leave for 5 minutes. Remove fish, skin and flake, removing any bones.) Reserve cooking liquid.

Boil the rice until tender in the water used to cook fish, topped up with fresh water as necessary. Drain and set aside. Fry the onion in the butter until soft. Add the fish, rice and eggs and mix well. Stir in the parsley, seasoning and cream and heat through. Serve immediately. Serves 4.

Baked Cod with savoury tomato sauce

Herbs, spices and tomatoes are used to flavour the oven-baked cod which makes a tasty meal when served with a fresh green salad. Any white fish may be used instead of the cod.

**1 lb. cod fillets   1 teaspoon paprika   1 egg   1 tablespoon olive oil
1 garlic clove, crushed   1 onion, chopped   1 small green pepper, deseeded & chopped
2-3 oz. streaky bacon, chopped   2 medium fresh tomatoes, peeled & chopped
1 tablespoon tomato purée   2 teaspoon dried thyme
2 teaspoon dried basil   5 fl. oz. dry white wine   8 pitted black olives
2 tablespoons chopped parsley   Salt & pepper to season**

Set oven to 350°F or Mark 4. Beat the egg and season with paprika. Ensure that the fish is dry by patting with kitchen paper. Dip each fish fillet into the beaten egg and place onto a greased baking tray. Bake uncovered in the oven for 15-20 minutes. To test if the fish is cooked through gently insert a sharp knife into the centre and if it flakes easily it is ready. Remove from the oven and keep warm. To make sauce, heat the olive oil in a large frying pan, add the onion, pepper, garlic and bacon and sauté for 5-10 minutes until soft. Stir in the tomatoes, herbs, tomato purée wine and olives; bring to the boil stirring continuously. Cover tightly and simmer gently for 10-15 minutes until all the vegetables are cooked. Transfer the cod onto warmed plates and spoon over sauce and serve with boiled rice. Serves 4.

Dawn Clouds at Penmon Lighthouse, Anglesey

Fish Soup

Fish soup can be made using fish according to the season and the catch.
There are many variations. This one derives from Brixham in Devon.

2 tablespoons olive oil   2 onions, peeled and sliced   2 cloves garlic, crushed
2 medium leeks, trimmed and sliced   2 medium carrots, peeled and sliced thinly
1 large can chopped tomatoes   1½ pints good fish stock
½ pint dry white wine   2 bay leaves   Salt and pepper
2 lb. mixed fish fillets (monkfish, gurnard, cod, plaice etc.)
4 tablespoons double cream   1 tablespoon chopped parsley

Heat the oil in a large saucepan, add the onions and fry until softened. Add the garlic, leeks and carrots and cook for 2-3 minutes. Add the tomatoes, stock, wine and bay leaves. Season and simmer for 15 minutes. Prepare the fish by cutting into bite-sized pieces. Add the firm fish first (for example monkfish) and cook for 3 minutes, then add the more delicate fish (for example plaice) and cook for a further 2 or 3 minutes. Do not overcook the fish. Pour the soup into a warmed dish, stir in the cream and sprinkle with parsley.

Skate with Black Butter

Skate is in season from September to April. The only parts eaten are the 'wings' which are sold whole from young skate or sliced from larger fish.

1½-2 lb. skate	**Court bouillon**
2 oz. butter	**2 teaspoons capers**
2 tablespoons wine vinegar	**2 teaspoons chopped parsley**

Salt & freshly ground black pepper

For court bouillon:
Simmer a carrot, an onion, a clove, a bouquet garni, 8 peppercorns and a pinch of salt in 2 pints of water and 2 tablespoons vinegar for 15-20 minutes. Strain.

Simmer the skate in the court bouillon for 15-20 minutes or until tender. Remove from pan, drain and dry on kitchen paper. Set aside and keep warm on a serving dish. Heat butter in pan until it turns a rich brown colour. Stir in the vinegar and capers and boil for 2-3 minutes to reduce slightly. Pour over the fish, sprinkle with the parsley and serve immediately. Serves 4.

Sussex Lobster or Crab Pie

The waters of the English Channel off Sussex provide fine lobsters and crabs
and these have long been a delicacy in the resort towns along the coast.

The meat from 2 medium-size fresh lobsters, approximately ½ lb. each (reserve contents of the heads and the coral) or 3 medium-size fresh crabs (reserve brown meat and treat same as lobster 'head and coral' meat)

8 oz. shortcrust pastry   ¼-½ pint single cream   2 hard-boiled eggs
Lemon juice   Seasoning   Ground mace   Butter

Set oven to 400°F or Mark 6. Line a 6½-7 inch greased baking tin with pastry. Place a layer of the crab meat on to the pastry. Season with salt, pepper and mace. Add a little lemon juice and dot with butter. Add a layer of sliced egg. Repeat layers with the remaining meat and eggs. Cover with a pastry lid. Cook for 40-45 minutes until the filling is sizzling. Meanwhile mix the head and coral meat with enough cream to make a sauce. When baked, lift the lid and pour the sauce over the contents. Replace lid. Serve with a green salad. A layer of oysters can be added, before baking, if desired. Serves 4-6.

Fishing Boat on Hastings Beach, East Sussex

Fish and Vegetable Stew

A light meal of creamy fish, stewed with vegetables.
Delicious served with fresh bread rolls.

1¼ lb. white fish fillets   1 lemon, quartered and sliced
2 tablespoons chopped fresh dill and a sprig for marinade
3 fl. oz. dry white wine   1 tablespoon lemon juice   Salt & pepper to season
4 medium carrots peeled and cut into 2 inch julienne strips
3 courgettes cut into 2 inch julienne strips   8 fl. oz. milk
1 tablespoon cornflour   2 celery sticks, chopped
2 tablespoons chopped fresh parsley
3 tablespoons double cream

Chop the fish into 1 inch pieces and put into a bowl with the dill sprig and sliced lemon. Cover with the wine and lemon juice and season to taste. Cover bowl and leave for at least 30 minutes to marinate. Place carrots and 7 fl. oz. of the milk in a medium saucepan and bring to the boil gently. Cover and simmer for 10 minutes, adding the courgettes after 5 minutes. Strain the marinade from the fish and add the liquid to the vegetables. Mix the cornflour with the remaining milk and add to the pan, heating gently, stirring until thickened. Add the marinated fish, lemons and celery and simmer gently for 5-6 minutes. Stir in the cream and chopped herbs, heat gently and serve. Serves 4.

Savoury Plaice Mornay

With orange spots on its upper side, plaice has a delicate flavour and soft flesh.
It is available all year round and can be bought whole or in fillets.

1 oz. butter   2 small onions, peeled & sliced thinly
4 oz. mushrooms, sliced   Grated rind of ½ lemon
1 tablespoon chopped parsley   8 plaice fillets
10 fl. oz. dry white wine   Salt & ground black pepper
2 egg yolks   4 tablespoons double cream
1 teaspoon cornflour   Pinch of freshly grated nutmeg
4 oz. grated cheese

Set oven to 350°F or Mark 4. Melt the butter in a large frying pan and soften the onions and mushrooms. Add the parsley, grated lemon rind, stir well and season to taste. Lay the plaice fillets out flat, top with the mixture and roll up. Place the rolls in an ovenproof dish and pour over the wine. Cover and cook for 30 minutes. Remove from the oven and strain off the cooking liquid. Beat the egg yolks, cream and cornflour together, and then blend in the fish liquid. Pour into a shallow pan and heat gently, stirring continuously until the sauce is thickened. Stir in the nutmeg and half the grated cheese. Spoon the sauce carefully over the fish and sprinkle with the rest of the cheese. Place under a preheated grill until the top is browned. Serves 4.

Creamy Finnan Haddie

Finnan Haddie is traditionally a lightly smoked and delicately flavoured haddock from the east coast of Scotland.

2 Finnan haddocks (divided into 4 pieces)
1 pint milk   2 oz. butter   2 tablespoons flour
2 heaped teaspoons dry mustard   5 fl. oz. double cream
Bay leaf   Pepper

Finnan Haddies have a lovely subtle flavour ideal for this dish; other smoked haddock, however, can be substituted, if necessary.

Place the fish in a large saucepan. Cover with the milk. Add the bay leaf and pepper. Bring to the boil. Reduce heat and simmer gently until the fish is cooked. Carefully lift the fish with a slice, drain and place in a heated shallow serving dish; cover with foil and keep warm. Strain the fish milk into a jug. Melt the butter in a saucepan. Stir in the flour and mustard. Cook for 2 minutes. Add the fish milk. Bring to the boil, stirring continuously until it thickens. Remove from the heat. Stir in the cream. Reheat the sauce but do not boil. Pour over the fish. Serve with boiled potatoes and a fresh green vegetable. Serves 4.

Fish Stuffed Pancakes

The size of pancakes can be varied according to personal preference
– one large or two smaller per person.

Filling:
1 lb. of mixed cooked fish & shellfish (e.g. haddock & prawns)   1½ oz. butter, melted
1½ oz. cornflour   ¾ pint milk   4 oz. grated Cheddar cheese
Pancakes:
4 oz. plain flour   Pinch of salt   2 medium eggs, beaten
½ pint milk   ½ tablespoon melted butter

Make the pancakes first by sieving flour and salt into a mixing bowl. Combine the eggs and milk and gradually beat into the flour. When ready to cook, add the melted butter and stir. Heat a little oil in a non-stick frying pan and add enough batter to form a thin coating. Cook until brown and crisp, turning and cooking the other side. Set pancakes aside and keep warm. Set oven to 400°F or Mark 6. Heat the butter in a saucepan and add the cornflour. Heat gently, stirring continuously for 1 minute. Gradually add milk and bring to the boil slowly, stirring well. Season to taste and add the grated cheese. Lower the heat and stir until the sauce is thickened. Mix ⅓ of the sauce with cooked fish, fill the pancakes and roll up. Spread a thin layer of sauce over the bottom of an ovenproof dish. Place the pancakes on top and cover with the remaining sauce. Cover and cook in preheated oven for about 30 minutes. Serves 4.

Creamy Cheese Haddock

A tasty light supper dish served on hot buttered toast.

1 lb. smoked haddock	10 fl. oz. milk
1½ oz. butter or margarine	4 oz. grated Cheddar cheese
4 tablespoons cornflour	Salt & freshly ground black pepper
Chopped flat leaf parsley	

Clean and trim the fish, lay in a pan and cover with water. Bring slowly to the boil. Remove from the heat, cover tightly and leave to stand for 10 minutes or until the fish is tender. Remove fish from the liquid, take off and discard the skin and flake the flesh. Reserve the cooking liquor. Melt the butter or margarine in a pan, stir in the cornflour and cook over low heat for 2-3 minutes stirring continuously. Remove from the heat and slowly stir in ¼ pint of the fish liquor and the milk. Slowly bring to the boil and stir until the sauce is thick. Remove from the heat and add the cheese and seasoning. Stir well and serve on buttered toast. Sprinkle with chopped parsley. Serves 4.

Fish Supper

When the fishing fleets came in, housewives would go down to the harbour and purchase the broken fish, not suitable for sale at the quay or fish market, using it to make a Fish Supper.

**2 mackerel, cleaned and filleted   1-1½ lb. cod or haddock fillets
2 oz. butter   1 large onion, peeled and chopped
1 teaspoon mace   ½ teaspoon turmeric   Salt and black pepper
1 pint water   1 small dressed crab or small tin of crabmeat (optional)
2 tablespoons chopped parsley   A little grated cheese**

Melt the butter in a deep saucepan and fry the onion until soft. Add the fish, spices and seasoning, then pour the water over. Bring to the boil then simmer for 20 to 30 minutes. Lift out the fish and onion with a slotted spoon and place in a warm, ovenproof serving dish. Drain the crabmeat well (if tinned), crumble and sprinkle over. Stir half the parsley into the stock and pour a little over the fish. Cover with foil and keep warm in a low oven. Just before serving, sprinkle with grated cheese and flash under the grill to melt. Sprinkle the remaining parsley and serve with boiled potatoes. Serves 4.

Blakeney Sunset, Norfolk

Spiced Cod

The combination of the spices and the fruit and chutney make a delicious crunchy topping to complement the taste of the fresh cod.

4 cod steaks	**1½ tablespoons sultanas**
1½ oz. butter	**1 tablespoon mango chutney**
1½ teaspoons curry powder	**Salt & pepper**
1 teaspoon Worcestershire sauce	**2 tablespoons fresh breadcrumbs**

Set oven to 375°F or Mark 5. Place cod steaks in a greased shallow ovenproof dish. Combine the remaining ingredients and spread evenly over the fish. Place in the preheated oven and bake uncovered for 20-25 minutes or until fish is cooked and easily flakes. Serves 4.

Cullen Skink

Cullen Skink is a thick Scottish soup traditionally made with smoked haddock, potatoes and onions.

1 large Finnan haddock	1 pint full cream milk or buttermilk
1 onion, chopped	1 oz. butter
½ lb. mashed potato	Salt and pepper

Place the haddock in a large pan with sufficient water to cover. Bring to the boil, add the chopped onion and simmer for 10-15 minutes until the fish is cooked. Remove the fish, retaining the stock, and flake the flesh from the bones and skin. Set the flesh to one side and return the bones and skin to the stock. Boil for 30 minutes. Remove from the heat and strain the stock into a clean pan. Add the flaked fish and return to the heat. Add the milk and salt to taste and bring to the boil for a few minutes. Stir in the mashed potato, butter and pepper to taste, and serve immediately. Serves 4.

Soused Herrings

*A popular way to serve herrings. The sharp taste of the marinade
is a perfect complement to the rich flesh of the fish.*

**4 medium herrings, fins, tails & backbones removed
Salt & ground black pepper   1 small onion, sliced
1 tablespoon pickling spice   5 fl. oz. malt vinegar
5 fl. oz. water**

Set oven to 300°F or Mark 2. Clean the herrings and pat dry. Season well with
salt and pepper. Roll up from head to tail, skin side out and secure using a
wooden cocktail stick. Arrange the fish in a shallow ovenproof dish and add
the onion, pickling spice, vinegar and water. Cover and bake in preheated oven
for 3 hours until the fish is tender. Remove from the oven and leave to cool in
cooking liquor, then chill in the refrigerator. Drain and remove cocktail sticks
before serving. Serves 4.

Savoury Fish Crumble

A fish pie with a difference, topped with a cheesy oat crumble.

1¼ lb. white fish fillets   10 fl. oz. milk   5 black peppercorns   1 bay leaf
Sauce:
3 tablespoons cornflour   1½ oz. butter   ½ lemon, squeezed for juice
2 tablespoons chopped flat leaf parsley   Salt & pepper to taste
Topping:
4 oz. flour   2½ oz. butter   1 oz. rolled oats   1 tablespoon grated Parmesan cheese

Set oven to 375°F or Mark 5. Poach the fish in the milk with the peppercorns and bay leaf for 7-8 minutes or until just cooked. Remove using a slotted spoon and put milk aside. Remove skin from fish and flake. For the sauce – melt the butter in a pan, stir in the cornflour and heat gently stirring for 2 minutes. Remove from the heat and slowly add the milk reserved from the poaching. Return to heat, slowly bring to the boil, stirring continuously and simmer for 1 minute. Remove from heat again, stir in lemon juice, parsley and fish. Season to taste. Pour into an ovenproof dish. To make the topping rub the flour and butter together and stir in the oats and cheese. Season to taste. Sprinkle over the fish sauce and bake in preheated oven for 30 minutes until the top is browned. Serves 4.

Whiting and Bacon Whirls

*This is a fishy twist to the more conventional cocktail
party sausages wrapped in bacon on a stick.*

**8 small whiting fillets skinned and dried   2 tablespoons flour
Salt & pepper   2 beaten eggs   4 oz. golden breadcrumbs
Oil or fat for frying
8 slices streaky bacon, rinds removed sliced lengthways**

Halve the fillets, coat in flour seasoned with salt and pepper. Dip in the beaten eggs and then roll in the breadcrumbs ensuring fish is thoroughly covered. Heat the oil in a non-stick frying pan and add the fillets, cooking for 4-8 minutes, turning to ensure all sides are browned. Carefully remove fish from the pan and wrap a slice of bacon around each, using a cocktail stick to secure. Put fillets back into pan and cook for 3-5 minutes, turning to ensure the bacon is crisp and cooked. Makes 16 whirls.

Dorset Crab Tart

A popular delicacy from the resort towns of Dorset,
this crab tart can be served warm or cold.

8 oz. shortcrust pastry

FILLING
4 oz. cream cheese   1 medium egg   ¼ pint single cream
2 teaspoons lemon juice   Salt and pepper
½ - ¾ lb. crab meat (mixture of white and brown meat)
4 spring onions, trimmed, washed and cut into ¼ inch slices
Watercress to garnish

Set oven to 400°F or Mark 6. Roll out the pastry on a lightly floured surface and use to line an 8-inch flan ring. Prick the base with a fork, line with cooking foil, and bake for 10-15 minutes. Remove the foil, put the cream cheese into a large bowl and beat until soft. Mix in the egg, cream, lemon juice and seasoning. Arrange the crab meat and spring onions over the base of the flan and pour over the cheese mixture. Reduce oven temperature to 375°F or Mark 5 and bake for 30-40 minutes until set and golden. Serve warm or cold and garnished with watercress. Serves 4.

Plaice and Prawn Supreme

This is an ideal dish to serve for a special evening meal with green vegetables. Plaice fillets are stuffed with herby cream cheese and combined with prawns in a delicately flavoured sauce. The dish is piped with a creamy mashed potato for that extra special touch.

4 large plaice fillets, skinned cut in half lengthways
¼ lb. herb & garlic cream cheese   Seasoning
½ lb. fresh peeled prawns   1 oz. butter   1 oz. cornflour
5 fl. oz. dry white wine   5 fl. oz. fish stock   2 oz. grated Emmenthal cheese
1 lb. potatoes (cooked and mashed with a knob of butter and 1 tablespoon milk)

Set oven to 375°F or Mark 5. Lay fillets skin side up and spread with herb & garlic cream cheese. Carefully roll fillets up and place in an ovenproof dish. Distribute prawns evenly over top and season to taste. To make the sauce, melt the butter in a small saucepan and add the cornflour stirring continuously over the heat for 2 minutes. Remove from the heat and gradually add the stock and wine ensuring that it is mixed well. Return to the heat and bring slowly to the boil, stirring continuously until thickened. Remove from the heat once more and mix in the grated cheese. Add sauce to the fish dish ensuring that everything is well covered. Pipe the mashed potato around the edge and bake in preheated oven for 30 minutes until the potato has browned. Serves 4.

Crumbed Cod Fingers

A quick and easy to make family favourite.

1 lb. skinless cod fillets	**2 tablespoons tomato pesto**
4 oz. fresh wholemeal breadcrumbs	**3 tablespoons flour**
1 oz. chopped flat leaf parsley	**2 medium eggs, beaten**

Set oven to 425°F or Mark 7. Slice the fish fillets into 12 strips of roughly the same size. Combine the pesto with the breadcrumbs and parsley in a shallow bowl. Put the flour and beaten eggs into 2 other bowls. Dip each fish piece into the flour, followed by the egg and lastly the breadcrumbs, ensuring that they are coated evenly. Place the fish on a greased baking sheet and cook in the preheated oven for 10 minutes until crispy and lightly browned. Serves 4.

Roast Sea Bass

The delicate flavour and texture of sea bass is becoming increasingly popular for home cooking. It is at its best cooked simply; either grilled, barbecued or roast as in this recipe.

1 large sea bass (or bream)	3 oz. suet
1 tablespoon chopped parsley	Salt
4 oz. breadcrumbs	Milk to mix

For the Parsley Butter:
2 oz. butter
1 tablespoon finely chopped parsley

Set oven to 400°F or Mark 6. Have the fish cleaned and scaled by the fishmonger. Keep back 1 oz. suet (for basting) and thoroughly mix the rest with the chopped parsley, breadcrumbs and a pinch of salt. Moisten with a little milk. Stuff the fish with this mixture and put into a greased baking dish. Sprinkle with the remaining suet and season generously with salt. Bake until golden brown, basting frequently and adding more suet if it seems at all dry. Serve with parsley butter made of 2 oz. butter and 1 tablespoon finely chopped parsley, well blended.

Haddock in Lemon Butter Sauce

A delicately flavoured dish. Cod can be used instead of haddock, if preferred.

4 haddock fillets or steaks, skinned
½ pint milk
Finely grated rind 1 lemon

Salt and pepper
1 tablespoon cornflour
2 tablespoons milk
1 oz. butter

Lemon slices to garnish

Place the haddock in a large frying pan with the milk and lemon rind. Season to taste and simmer gently for 8 minutes or until the fish is tender. Carefully transfer the fish to a serving dish and keep warm. Blend the cornflour with the two tablespoons of milk and stir into the pan with the butter. Bring to the boil, whisking all the time until the sauce is thick and smooth. Spoon the sauce over the fish and serve immediately, garnished with lemon slices. Serves 4.

Fish Hotpot

White fish layered in a casserole, with potatoes and mushrooms with a cheese sauce.

1 lb. cod (or any white fish of your choice) skinned and cut into 1 inch pieces

Seasoned flour	**1 medium sized onion, finely chopped**
1½ lb. boiled potatoes	**¼ pint white sauce**
1 tablespoon lemon juice	**4 oz. grated cheese**
4 oz. mushrooms, sliced	**Salt and pepper**

Chopped parsley or chives for decoration

Set oven to 400°F or Mark 6. Well grease a deep casserole dish with butter. Toss the fish in seasoned flour. Slice the potatoes thinly; arrange half the potatoes on the base of the dish, then layer with the fish sprinkled with the lemon juice, then the mushrooms, onions and seasoning. Add 2 oz. of the grated cheese to the white sauce and pour over the mixture. Top with the rest of the potatoes. Sprinkle with the remainder of the cheese and bake, uncovered, for 40 minutes. Just before serving, sprinkle with the chopped parsley or chives. Serves 4.

METRIC CONVERSIONS

The weights, measures and oven temperatures used in the preceding recipes can be easily converted to their metric equivalents. The conversions listed below are only approximate, having been rounded up or down as may be appropriate.

Weights

Avoirdupois	Metric
1 oz.	just under 30 grams
4 oz. (¼ lb.)	app. 115 grams
8 oz. (½ lb.)	app. 230 grams
1 lb.	454 grams

Liquid Measures

Imperial	Metric
1 tablespoon (liquid only)	20 millilitres
1 fl. oz.	app. 30 millilitres
1 gill (¼ pt.)	app. 145 millilitres
½ pt.	app. 285 millilitres
1 pt.	app. 570 millilitres
1 qt.	app. 1.140 litres

Oven Temperatures

	°Fahrenheit	Gas Mark	°Celsius
Slow	300	2	150
	325	3	170
Moderate	350	4	180
	375	5	190
	400	6	200
Hot	425	7	220
	450	8	230
	475	9	240

Flour as specified in these recipes refers to plain flour unless otherwise described.